# FRONTIER TALES

Juanita Brooks

# FRONTIER TALES
## TRUE STORIES OF REAL PEOPLE

Western Text Society
Special Publication
Logan, Utah

Library of Congress Number 72-93748
ISBN: 0-47421-053-4
© 1972 Utah State University Press

# CONTENTS

# SAM'S COURTSHIP

Sam came to Utah with the first Swiss Company of 1861. He traveled with the family of a married brother, taking his place at the handcart shafts, which left the wife to follow with the children and help push from behind on the up-hill places. Their experiences were shared by all who came to Zion in this most trying journey.

In Salt Lake City they had a time to rest before starting on south to their destination. Here they left their handcarts, to be transported on by wagon teams of settlers. Before they left, Brother Brigham called them together and advised young couples who were "keeping company" to get married. Young men of marriageable age should look around for congenial mates, for they would be far from headquarters. In that hard land a man would need the support of a wife.

This idea did not appeal to Sam at all. He did not intend to get married just to be married. He would wait until he found a girl he really wanted, even though he was the only young man over twenty-one years of age who was not married. When the land was divided into lots in Santa Clara, he was given one along with the other adult men.

His lot was on the north side of the road, with the point of a hill jutting down into it, a gravelly, rocky lot. But it was his, and he would make something of it. He and his brother shared work, helping each other on the lots and in the field. By the spring of 1863 Sam had built himself a neat dugout room inside the jutting hill. He shoveled back and squared off the sides until he had a 12 by 14 floor space, with a rock fireplace set in the back. He worked carefully here to make the front and mantel beautiful and to build the chimney tall enough to insure a good draught.

He built up the slanting sides and made the front wall of rock set in lime mortar. His door-frame was wood, the door itself of heavy plank, with a square hole for light. He had no glass, so he rigged up an inside "plug" of board hung on hinges of rawhide, with a leather tab in the other end to fasten to a nail above when he wanted the window open. The walls on both sides of the fireplace were squared off to make benches, with other niches higher up for lamps or toilet articles.

He had it almost ready to move into when he was called to take an outfit from Santa Clara to meet the spring emigration and bring them in. Handcarts had been abandoned. Teams would haul the goods and supplies of the emigrants, but all who were able to do so were expected to walk—except on the downhill grades.

Sam's outfit consisted of his horse and one of his brother's, a wagon belonging to a neighbor, and supplies from the entire village. He joined other outfits from the settlements north until there was a full train of twenty wagons, carrying supplies.

The trip out was without incident. The emigrants arrived on schedule and the work of organizing was carried out with dispatch. Sam was near the supply wagons for a company from Switzerland, but ate and camped with the teamsters, separate from the Swiss. So far as he knew, he was the only teamster who spoke German.

After a few days on the road, the travel fell into a regular pattern. The loaded wagons carrying Church goods pulled

2

out ahead, and the other wagons fell into line, while the emigrants walked on one side or the other, sometimes ahead on the up-hill stretches. Every day a group of Swiss girls would pass his wagon, eight of them, visiting and laughing and often knitting as they walked. Sam looked them over carefully, but said not a word. Within a week he had decided that one of them was extra-special. But how to approach her?

On the up-hill stretches, the drivers walked beside the team. One morning Sam had let his horses stop to rest, and the girls came along laughing and joking. He thought he heard a German phrase, "Dumber than an ox." He quickly answered in German, saying that anyone who had only horses to talk to all day long would seem dumber than an ox.

The girls squealed and laughed with embarrassment, but Sam was suddenly brave. He spoke out clearly in German.

"Why don't one of you come and walk with me for a while? Maybe, just maybe, I'm not so dumb after all."

The girls all hesitated, uncertain what to do.

"You in the blue dress there! Why don't you come?"

She made no move, but the others encouraged her and pushed her out toward him, while they all ran on ahead, wondering how much this fellow had heard of their conversation at other times.

Sam asked her name, and when she didn't answer, he said, "That's all right. I've already named you. I call you *Antoinette,* because you carry yourself like a queen. But I've shortened it to *Nettie.* That's my name for you from now on."

He didn't ask further about her, but proceeded to tell her about himself—where he was born in Switzerland, his family, and their joining the Church, and the mission to Dixie. Here he grew eloquent: a little Switzerland, this village. Here they had a Singing School one night a week where they sang their own German songs, and learned some new ones, a few in English. Then there was the Band! Brother Staheli had an inheritance in his old home town, which couldn't be paid in

3

cash, so he accepted band instruments instead. Trumpets, trombones, bass horn and baritones—a full set. True, they had little music as yet, except that which Brother Staheli wrote out for them, but they still had the best music in all the southern part of the Territory.

And the people were so neighborly, and so helpful and industrious.

"Then look at me," he said jokingly. "I'm not in bad shape myself. And I've got a lot of my own and a snug little house on it, and a piece of farm land in the field that belongs to me. This mare here is mine; I have a heifer that will be a cow this fall. What I need most is a good wife to work along with me and help me take care of what I do have. At least I don't owe anyone anything."

When she seemed not too impressed, he broke forth into a short love-song in German. The noon stop call sounded.

"Well, I'll see you again tomorrow, I hope. Or if you don't want to come, don't; and I'll pick one of the others. But just remember that from the first time I saw you, I picked you for my choice. 'Bye for now, Nettie. See you tomorrow."

So it was that every day as the girls walked ahead of the wagons, Nettie stopped, sometimes for only a few minutes and sometimes for all forenoon.

When at last they had crossed the Great Divide and had down-hill going, he persuaded her to climb onto the wagon and ride beside him on the spring-seat.

"You should see how wonderful it is up here. You can see miles and miles in every direction." So she took his hand and climbed up.

It was much easier to talk to her now, with both sitting on the spring-seat side by side. Now he could tell her more about the Swiss village in Utah. He explained that the hills were different—red and bare—but beautiful in the morning and evening. And the summer was hot, but the mild winter made up for that. And the people! Well, better people could not

4

be found anywhere, the world over.

During all these weeks she had said little about herself, her family, or how it was that she was here without her parents. He wondered if perhaps she had her heart set on a missionary here in Zion. He had seen other girls get ogle-eyed over the missionaries before he left Switzerland; he had watched how one or two always managed to run into a certain Elder, and not entirely by accident.

But he didn't ask. He just kept on cheerfully entertaining her with little jokes and bits of verse, and English words and phrases that would be handy for her to know. This really interested her; she would repeat the words over and over, and make a game out of trying to converse in English.

As they neared Salt Lake City, he stopped trying to court her. Instead, he pointed out some of the landmarks that he knew, and explained about Emigration Square, where friends always came to meet their families and neighbors from the Old Country. He could see her excitement mount as they drove through the City and he explained about the Council House, the Tithing Office and *Deseret News* Building and the stores and shops, with the big signs, and the carriages and carts and loaded wagons everywhere.

He wanted to hold her hand a little; to show a bit of affection, but she was looking all the time for someone in the crowd. At last they stopped in Emigration Square, where some of the Authorities were gathered on a platform, and people milled around in crowds.

Now Sam said to her seriously. "This wagon leaves for Dixie at six o'clock Monday morning. If you want to go with it, you be here before that time. You will have a little more than three days in the city."

He thought she was too eager to jump off the wagon and join her girl-friends. They remained in a group, all hoping they would see a familiar face among the crowd which was gathering.

5

On Monday morning Sam was up early so that he could give his horses a feed of grain and a drink of water before he hitched up. As he led them back to harness them, he saw that Nettie was sitting on the spring-seat, her trunk of clothing and bed roll in the wagon. His heart jumped into his throat, but he tried not to appear excited.

"Hi! Good-morning," he called out. "Glad to see you!"

The wagons were already forming into line, so he pulled over into his place and followed at the required distance, so that the dust of the wagon ahead would not be too heavy on his.

He wondered how she had spent her three days here, and if she had found Zion all she expected it to be. He wondered who she had stayed with, and how she had fared. Across the plains, the food had been hauled in wagons and issued to the travelers according to the number in each mess. The teamsters from the south had drawn supplies from the general Tithing Office and had cards to the Bishops along the way, asking them to supply food for the travelers and their teams.

Sam was so full of love and joy that he could hardly wait to get out on the open road where he could sing, yodel, and put his arm around Nettie and pull her close and kiss her cheek. She laughed at his jokes and antics, and even sang some herself to fill in the time. At noon when he pulled out his grub-box, he found that she also had some food—sandwiches, boiled eggs, cookies and fruit that friends in Zion had provided for her. A regular picnic, this meal!

They had a short noon stop, for they hoped to reach Lehi to camp, though it would make a very long day. It was dark as they neared the town, and just outside it they passed an Indian camp beside the road—not a large camp, but about a half-dozen braves with their squaws and papooses. Nettie was terrified. She crowded close to Sammy and said, almost in tears, "Oh, Sammy, let's get married tonight!"

This was what Sammy had been waiting for. He had not

discussed marriage at all; she had been so silent and offish when he had tried to court her earlier, that it was now her turn to propose. With a hearty "O.K.!" he pulled off the road and stopped the team. He had just time for a squeeze and a kiss as a horseman came by.

"Can you direct me to the home of the Bishop here?" Sam asked, and was pleased that it was just around the corner. He pulled over and stopped the wagon near the corral, unharnessed his team, watered and fed them, as a true frontiersman would. On the road, a man's first consideration must be his horses. He washed his hands and face at the watering trough, combed his hair carefully, brushed himself off the best he could, and joined Nettie, who had also made her toilet. Together they went to the door. Their knock brought the Bishop's wife, wiping her hands on her apron.

"Is the Bishop in?" Sam asked.

Mrs. Bishop had opened the door with her left hand because her right one was covered with flour.

"Sit down and make yourselves comfortable. He'll not be long," she said cheerfully.

From where she sat, Nettie could see that the Bishop's wife was working some flour in a large bowl, dropping a few drops of milk into it and pressing it through her fingers as if to dampen it without making it sticky. Soon she began to rub it between her two hands, and then as the milk in the large kettle began to boil, she stirred the dampened flour into it. The "lumpy" quality now was very evident. Not lumps like small dumplings, but more like the size of kernels of corn, in a thick mixture. She covered the kettle and pushed it to the back of the stove where it could cook slowly without scorching.

The Bishop was very cordial and understanding. He talked to the young people, assured himself that they were both of legal age and responsible before the law, and made out the proper forms giving age and date and place of birth of each. He called in a neighbor to stand as one witness, while his wife stood as the other, and he read the ceremony clearly and with proper emphasis. After the first kiss as man and wife, Sam was ready to leave, but Mrs. Bishop interfered.

"Why don't you take your wedding supper with us?" she asked. "We have only lumpy-dick, but it's hot, and there's plenty of it. We'd be right glad to have you."

So Sam and Nettie were introduced to this pioneer dish, "lumpy-dick," the standard supper meal in many a frontier home.

Sam took hay from the Bishop's stack to put into the wagon-box for a mattress, and with their combined bed-rolls they could be very comfortable. They pulled the wagon-cover down tight to keep out the wind and to insure privacy.

On the road next day Nettie started looking for a house that would be something like the snug little place Sam had boasted about when they first met.

"Is our house like that?" she would ask again and again as they traveled along, but not once did she find one that was like it. All the way along it was the same: there was no house quite like his.

Sam planned to arrive in Santa Clara late at night and sleep in the wagon-box as usual. Before daylight the next morning he slipped out of bed, pulled on his pants and shoes, and started down the street to his lot and the little dug-out home. He had been away more than six months, and he knew that the weeds would be thick and high. He had left his shovel there, and expected to clear around the house before he brought Nettie to see it.

But she was not asleep. He had hardly stepped off the wagon tongue before she raised up to see what direction he was going. She quickly dressed and followed.

Sam hurried to the place, but HORRORS! ! There had been a very recent cloud-burst and a stream from the hill had run around the fireplace chimney, caved in the roof, and pushed the whole front of the house down flat on its face!

Sam just dropped down on a log and buried his face in his hands. After all his build-up about the house, what could he say to her now? He didn't get a chance to say anything, for she stepped up behind him, sat down on the log and put her arm around his shoulders.

"Why Sam, it IS a beautiful house! See that lovely fireplace! It's all safe and sound. Get another shovel and let me help. We can have it fixed in no time, and we'll put a glass window in! There were some in the freight, you know, and you may take part of your pay from that. Don't worry! We'll soon have it fixed, and before we're through we'll have a home as nice as any in this whole town!"

"You wonderful girl," Sam said, taking her into his arms and holding her tight. "Of course we can fix it, but we can't get it done this morning before breakfast. I think we should go back to the house. The family will be getting up and I want them to meet my new wife. Won't they be surprised, though! They'll want to give us a wedding party, I'm sure."

Sam was right. The family loved Nettie on sight; they were pleased and proud that such a lovely girl as this should choose Sam. This was Friday morning. The word went out that Sam had come home with a bride, and most of the village already knew of the condition of his house. Hadn't he gone out to represent them all? Shouldn't they do some little thing to repay this in part? How about if every man gave a half-day's work on Sam's house and lot. They would make a "bee" of it, and the women could all contribute to a wedding supper in the evening, at the meeting house. They could have a bit of a program and a dance after. The work could be their wedding present, but if some cared to bring other gifts, they would be welcome, of course.

"Many hands make work light," the German proverb says.

9

So it was that Sam's lot was cleared of weeds, the rocks gathered into piles near the street where they might later be put into a rock wall.

The repair of the house was a much more complicated piece of work. Though it could not be finished, it took on a basic form that Sam could take his own time to complete.

The dinner was ample; there was singing and music and dancing; there was a pause while Sam led his bride around the room and introduced her to every person in the house. Now she was really one of the community.

## II

Though it took a little time, Sam's house was greatly improved by the rebuilding: in fact, it was good enough to last until he could build a permanent home. A glass window of eight panes was in the east side; a single pane was in the front door; the floor was covered with flagstones filled in between with mortar; the benches that were cut out on the sides were also mortared over. The "cat-hole" in the front door hung on two leather straps, so that it would open out, but not in—which meant that the cat or dog could go out as they wished, but would have to be invited back—or at least permitted to come in.

Among the wedding gifts were a coal-oil lamp, some assorted tinware, a braided rug, four porcelain plates (one each from four women), some home-made soap, a pincushion, and assorted hand-made doilies. All-in-all, Nettie felt that she had received a royal welcome here.

So many things they needed, but of one she was sure. Sam's hat was a wreck! There was no place here to buy a hat, and no money to pay for one. Nettie heard that "Auntie", an older lady who lived in a small house by herself, knew how to braid straw and sew it into hats. So taking some fresh-baked little biscuits, she went to call.

She was surprised that Auntie was so cheerful, so happy to see her, so eager to help. Auntie explained that to make hats, you must be very careful in your selection of the straw; then it must be soaked, but not too long; next it must be braided in a flat strand about an inch-and-a-half wide or wider. Nettie looked at the hats Auntie had there—three of them, but they were ladies' hats trimmed with colored straw shaped into flower-like decorations, which they called "artificials."

Nettie got the general idea and practiced until she had a braid about twelve inches long. Then she went to gather some straw for herself and take it home, determined to make Sam a hat.

She really labored at this, braiding a yard or so at a time and sewing it into a circle. From the first, she couldn't get it going right; it wouldn't spread out, but pulled in until it was more like a cone than a hat—unless it might be a Chinese hat. Finally she did get the braid into position to start a brim. Every time she stopped to press it into shape and study it, she would be tempted to either pick it all apart up to the last stitch or throw it away and start over. But she did neither. Having set herself to do it, she would finish this hat if Sam never once put it on. Next time she would know better how to begin.

Finally, after another long forenoon working at it, she decided that she would do no more. True, it looked crazy, but it would keep off the sun. She'd wait until after lunch to bring it out and show Sam, and if he refused to wear it, she wouldn't blame him.

"Look, Sam," she said, lifting the cloth that she had thrown over it, "I've had a bad time with this, and it's funny-looking, but I'm not going to throw it away. I'll start another one this afternoon."

"This is a very nice hat, a beautiful hat," Sam said, pushing it down on his head. "All it needs is a chin-strap to hold it on."

11

So Sam got a long buckskin string, took it around the crown, through at the sides, to tie on securely under his chin. It really wasn't so bad, after all. "This will start a new style in town," he said. "All the girls will be coming for the pattern."

Sam had left his horses to feed in the pasture, since he had no hay yet in the corral. This meant that he must walk the mile-and-a-half back to the field.

He had just got through town when an emigrant wagon pulled up beside him and the driver called out, "What'll you take for that hat?"

"One silver dollar," Sam answered promptly.

With the money in his hand, he hurried back home. Nettie didn't see him until he was at the door.

"You're in business, my girl!" he sang out. "Here, take that, and get what you need for baby-clothes! Or on the other hand, you might start a hat factory! I'll be your model and prize salesman."

Why should a girl start to cry at such good news? Nettie had never cried before. And as he took her into his arms, Sam knew that the tears were tears of joy at this unexpected turn of events.

He picked up his old hat from the trash pile he had deposited it on when he first came home, and went back to the field, whistling, and keeping in step with his own brisk tune.

# THE BUCKSKIN PANTS

The boy in this story is Thomas Watters Cropper, called Tom for short. He was the eldest of his mother's four children, and was raised on a large plantation in Texas, where they had many horses, cattle, hogs, about 100 stands of bees, and very much land. They also had Negro slaves, several of whom they brought along when they moved to Utah. This they did after his Father died and his Mother joined the Mormon Church in the early spring of 1856.

They traveled slowly because of the herd of cattle and band of horses they had along, staying in Holden in 1856 and 1857, because of the large open meadows and good feed for their animals. By 1863 they were living in the town of Washington, in the very southern-most corner of the state. They were asked to settle here because they were from the South, and knew something about raising and handling cotton. Since this area was known as "The Dixie Cotton Mission," they would be right at home here.

In the year of 1863 the people of the Cotton Mission raised more cotton than they knew what to do with. They had no mill to work it into cloth, no wire to bale it, no sacks to put it into. So they decided to make up a wagon train and haul it to the Missouri River, where the Church agent would be able to handle it. They packed it into their double-bedded wagons, pressing it down to crowd in as much as they could, then putting their hay and sacks of grain for the horses on top, along with their own grub-boxes, bedding and clothing. They would bring back machinery for the new cotton factory which was being started. Tom was to drive one of the teams, for he was an expert with horses. According to his account, other teams were going to bring in emigrants, so that the total number of wagons was seventy-eight. They were divided into two sections.

At this time Tom was nineteen years old and had out-grown most of his clothes. His mother could hardly believe how in one season he could put on so much height and weight. Clearly he must have a new outfit, or a pair of pants, at least. So she hired Sister Anderson to weave a "Frame" of cloth large enough to make them. Sister Anderson had already on hand thread which she had made from the cotton-bolls she had gleaned the year before, carded, and spun onto the spindles—a whole season's labor.

Next she threaded the loom with the required length, and wove it closely to make a strong fabric of good texture, sturdy enough to wear a long time. Last of all, she dyed it a yellow-green with rabbit-brush dye.

Now Tom's Mother took over, for she was an experienced tailor. She realized that these pants should last a long time, so she made them with generous seams, and an extra turn-up on the bottom. Every part was finished with great skill; she wanted her son to have a piece of clothing here that he could be proud to wear anywhere—in church, at a dance, or in the city.

Tom appreciated the pants, too. He had them carefully folded in a box, along with his Sunday shirt, clean underwear and sox, so that they would be ready when he needed them. He could travel as well in his regular patched work clothes.

"Patch upon patch, and a hole in the middle," was a

common folk saying. Tom's weren't that bad, but they were really well mended.

The other teamsters were married men or older fellows, each driving his own outfit. Though Tom was younger, he was large for his age and an expert at handling horses, so there was no reason why he should not make this trip. He ate with two older men, and was sociable enough with them, but when the train stopped outside the first city, he went by himself to bathe and clean up before he went into town. A good scrubbing, a shampoo and his clean, new outfit made him feel self-confident and fine as he started out. Then at one side, sitting on a log, were two of the older fellows from the second half of the train.

"Hi, kid! Where did you get them pants?" one sang out.

"I'll bet his Ma made 'em," the other chipped in. "Some color, that, ain't it? It would knock your eyes out. Otta be a law against a color like that on the street!"

They called him over and discussed his pants until he was quite embarrassed. He hardly knew what to do, or how to get away.

"Tell you what!" the first guy said. "I'll trade ye this pair o' buckskin pants for 'em. Twenty dollars a pair for buckskin pants, and they're all-the-go everywhere. They'll fit you to a *T*, I'll bet. You're big fer your age. Why don't you try 'em, jist fer fun, to see how they look? See how it'd feel to have some real man-sized buckskins. There's no wear-out to buckskins!"

So Tom took off his pants and handed them over. The other fellow took his time to pull off his buckskins. Then without waiting at all he quickly pulled on Tom's pants, and with a "Thank you, kid," he hurried away before Tom even got his feet into the buckskins. They were so stiff that he had quite a struggle to pull them up into place.

Horrors! They didn't fit where they touched, and they touched in all the wrong places. They had been wet and dried

15

and wet and dried until they could almost stand alone. The knobs on the knees came high up on his legs and the bottom hit the middle of his calf. They made him look bow-legged, and besides, the be-hind was too full.

So here he was, all alone. The two men were already out of sight and the camp deserted. Why had he been such a fool? Why didn't he just go right past and pay no attention to them?

Yes, here he was, soul alone. Too old to cry and too young to fight. He couldn't chase the guy down and get his pants back; that would make a scene, and he'd be the laughing stock of the camp. He could complain to the captain when he got back, but what good would that do? It would only make fun for the whole camp. Besides, his own pants would be all out of shape and soiled.

He went back into his wagon, took off the buckskin pants, pulled on his worn patches, and sat in complete dejection, angry at himself and helpless. What could be worse than to be without pants? Then as he looked at these hateful buckskin pants, he suddenly had an idea! He knew what he could do! He'd show them! But no one should know until his plan worked out. He'd just keep his mouth shut.

He started for the river bank with his camp hatchet in his hands. Selecting ten willows of uniform size, he cut and placed them in a pile. Then with his sharp pocket knife he trimmed and shaped and cut them to a uniform length of about two-and-a-half feet, and brought them to the wagon. Next he cut the pants apart, following the seams carefully and spreading them out to see how to get the most out of them. He would make one whip today, and prepare for the future, because he somehow wanted to carry out his project without the comments of the men. Eight very small strips from the straight seam of the buckskin pants; a heavy block of wood to fasten them to with a small nail, a great deal of care to get the strands started right. Soon the lash began to grow under his hands, smooth and round and perfect. The ends were tied, the fringe put on, and the whole fastened securely to the small end of a willow. Perfect! A bull whip well worth the two dollars he would ask for it! And all done in one long afternoon.

He would not finish another today. Instead he would prepare the eight strands for three or four more whips, tying each in a separate bunch, and rolling the extra buckskin away out of sight. During the long miles when the team would plod along without much direction, he could do the braiding. At the camps he could finish the whips and assemble the material for new ones.

Next he must make a sign to put on the side of his wagon. It took some figuring, but he managed it—a clear, bright, WHIPS FOR SALE $2.00. He sold his whips almost as fast as he could make them, so that by the time they reached the next city, he had twenty dollars in his pocket. He felt as rich as Croesus!

The next morning he went into town all scoured up, but in his old clothes. He didn't care. His head was high and his heart light—but he would look out and not be taken in by another shyster. At last he found a clerk who appealed to him, a boy a little older than he, but about the same size, who seemed to take a special interest in fitting him out. Finally Tom spent his money like this: a suit—pants and coat—in a good, solid fabric, $12.00; shoes, $2.00; socks, 15c; shirt, 85c; all high quality clothes.

Tomorrow he would shop for trinkets for his little brother and sister and something for the house. Maybe he could get enough scraps to make one more whip with a longer willow and a shorter lash. No, he'd go instead to the field where men were busy at the harvest, and ask for work. He would be a good field hand.

The clerk wrapped his old clothes neatly to take back, for Tom wanted to walk about the city looking as well dressed as the best of them. As he neared the camp, he saw from the corner of his eye, his pants! The two fellows were sitting on a log much the same as when he had seen them first. Tom walked straight ahead, pretending not to know they were there.

"Hey, Kid!" the man sang out. "Where did you get *that* outfit?"

"Who wants to know?" Tom answered in a clear voice. "I traded my buckskin pants for it!"

We should end the story here, but it seems worthwhile to add that the next morning Tom was back in his patched outfit, and out helping in the harvest field, while most of the men were playing cards or pitching horse shoes at the camp. Five dollars a day for four days, Tom earned. Of this he spent four dollars to buy a trunk in which to carry home his new clothes and his gifts for the family. But his greatest pride was in the suit that he had exchanged his buckskin pants for.

# A YOUNG BUSINESS MAN ON THE TRAIL

Gottleib Blickenstorfer was the only child of his parents, and he was born after his mother was forty years old. Like so many other folks in Switzerland, his parents joined the Mormon Church. They liked the doctrine, yes; but they also liked the idea of free land and open spaces and new opportunities in the Land of Zion. They loved and admired the young missionaries who told them about this new Church—pleasant young men, usually hungry, but very positive about the gathering to Zion while there was yet time. By all signs, the Second Coming could not be too far in the future.

By selling their home and most of their belongings, the Blickenstorfers had enough to pay their passage to America. While the Perpetual Emigration Plan was fine, they didn't want to be bound to work for a year to anyone—not at their age. Their son, Gottleib, now seventeen years old, was all excitement at the prospect of this trip to Zion, a land of great opportunity.

The ocean trip was fairly good, except for the Mother, who remained in her bunk most of the time. The ride on the train was better, so that by the time they had reached the

Mississippi River she felt confident that she would be able to make the trip on to Zion.

Handcarts had been abandoned. Church wagons carried the freight and baggage of the immigrants, but they themselves must walk.

For Gottlieb, this was fun. He was a healthy, husky lad, with red-gold hair and the red-brown eyes that often go with it, and an outgoing disposition, with a smile for everyone. Part of his confidence was inspired by the fact that he had with him two useful tools: a harmonica and a good pocket knife. He did not display these, but they gave him self-confidence. As he walked along, he kept a lookout for interesting pieces of wood, small boards, or twisted limbs. Sometimes he could see in one a hidden figure which his knife might uncover as he sat by the evening fire. Every night he would be working with his pocket knife, sometimes quite late. Then he would slip the item into the knapsack which he carried over his shoulder. After everyone else was in bed, and he himself flat on his back, he would play his harmonica softly, for he knew that his Mother would enjoy the music, whether anyone else heard it or not. Always he closed with a melody from the homeland.

After a short time, his mother began to fail. She simply could not keep up with the wagons. For the first hour she would walk along quite well, and then she would have to rest. Once Gottlieb and his father made a chair with their hands and carried her along. That was good for crossing streams and helping over rough places, but neither of them was able to keep the pace long.

One day a teamster asked Gottlieb if he was responsible for the music each night; he enjoyed it very much, he said. The boy was so happy to find one person with whom he could communicate a little, for each understood a few words of the other.

Gottlieb brought out one of the nicest little figurines he

had made; the teamster was much impressed and wanted to see others. One, especially, he really liked. How much money? he tried to ask.

"No money, No money at all. You let my Mother ride in the wagon a little time each day. She is not very heavy; but she is too weak to walk all the time. Maybe if the Captain sees her not, she can ride over the hardest places."

So his Mother started out to walk each morning, and at the first rest stop for the horses, she was lifted into the wagon. At noon she would start again, and again be picked up and put into the wagon. On the down-hill stretches she could always ride.

The knapsack was soon too heavy for him to carry all day, so for another clever little toy, the driver let him set it on top of the load near the back. Now his Mother could sort-of keep her eyes on it as they traveled, and he could add other items to it as he happened to find them. There were no houses along the prairie, but Gottleib knew that there would be opportunities in Zion. After all, the city would be about twelve years old by now; certainly there would be many people there who would like to buy some of his toys.

He was right. As they came to the outskirts of town where there were farm homes, he began to plan how he would proceed; then as they came through the thickly settled business section and stopped at Emigration Camp, he knew that he could find good markets for his wares. They would be here about three weeks, the emigrants were told.

Gottleib planned his work. He would not go out to sell until evening, for now that he could get some of the items that he needed—tacks, and cloth, and thin boards—he could work making things during the day. In the late afternoon, he would set out to sell. He would go to the back of the house, sit on the kitchen steps, and start to play his harmonica. If no one came out after two tunes, he left, and went to another place. Usually, though, the door opened quickly, before he had finished his first piece. He probably didn't sense that he was a very fine-looking, clean young man, who gave no appearance of a beggar.

Sometimes he was invited inside, taken into the living room, and invited to play another number. Most of these people were without any musical instrument in the home, and all were music-hungry. Sometimes they would ask him to come another night when they could invite their neighbors in and have a little party of music and singing. This would give him an opportunity to display samples of his handwork.

Sometimes people offered him food, but he always refused to eat it there. He would rather take it back to the camp, where his parents were staying. His Mother was not well, he would explain in his broken English; his Father was worn out with the long trip on foot—they both needed food. He would like to share with them. In this way he usually got a loaf of bread, some butter, jam, eggs, or other items which the land-lady could spare. During his stay in Salt Lake City he col-lected food to last for the rest of the journey to Dixie.

He practiced his English carefully, carrying with him a little German-English dictionary, pronouncing phrases and repeating them again and again until he could communicate quite well.

He was especially eager to get empty spools; there were so many things he could make if he had spools. One spool would make an excellent top, after he had whittled it down and inserted a good center with a spinning point on the bot-tom and knob on top. Or he could cut the spool in half and have wheels for a little cart. Two spools would fit out a little wagon.

So he would ask about little boxes, pieces of string or twine, scraps of cloth, either white or colored. Occasionally a good-hearted lady would let him select small pieces from her scrap bag.

His best line, of course, were the little items that he had

carved out on the way. While a top would be worth only ten cents, these figurines would range from twenty-five cents to a dollar. He soon was keenly sensitive about their relative value, for some were very nice, so nice, indeed, that he hated to part with them.

He knew that here in the city would be the best outlet for his wares. Here there were some wealthy people, many well-to-do ones also, who would not hesitate to buy anything that they took a fancy to. From them he asked cash, all in silver coins which he carried in a leather pouch with a drawstring on top.

He built up a surprising trade during the three weeks they were in the city. One lady asked him to come and entertain at an evening party to which she had invited two other families. He played his harmonica, doing some of the hymns where the crowd sang along with him; then playing solos of some favorite German songs, which they loudly applauded.

At the end he displayed some of his hand work on a stand in the center of the room. This brought forth astonished "How lovely!" exclamations from the audience. Many bought items; others asked if he would hold a special piece until they could get the cash. He early learned from the teamster on the plains that, while he might play his harmonica for food, and exchange the toys for spools, boxes, string or cloth, he must have cash for these original creations. They were worth money, and more than he realized.

His success in the city made him work all the harder on his way to Santa Clara. One special project, an intricate little jewel box, he kept for himself, until he should meet a girl— the right girl—many years hence.

You have guessed it, I know. By the time Gottleib arrived at Santa Clara he had enough money in his leather bag to buy a horse. Now a horse is half a team, and with a neighbor's harness and plow, he could plow up his own garden spot and one for his neighbor. Before the vegetables were ready for sale, he had built a one-horse cart from which to peddle them, exchanging them for whatever his customers had that he could use.

Money makes money, he learned. And a builder may build his home to his own specifications. So Gottleib and his father built a very nice little home of four rooms with porches front and back, and a cellar underneath. They planted shrubs and flowers around the house, and filled all the back lot with fruit trees, planting berries along the fence. Of course there was a vegetable garden, a cow, pigs, chickens, and ducks.

Although his mother was content in Zion, she seemed unable to regain her health, and after three years she died. His father, who needed a woman in the home, married a fine neighbor woman, who had some property of her own.

Though he was not yet twenty-one years of age, Gottleib struck out for himself, for now he had not only a team, but a wagon, a lot in town, and a piece of land in the field.

One Sunday when the Authorities came to Santa Clara and wanted to ride among the fields to see how people were getting along, they were surprised at what this very young man had accumulated.

"You must have had an inheritance from the Old World," one said. "You couldn't have got all this by yourself."

"I didn't get it by myself. I had two good friends to help me along the way. Without them I would not have done nearly so well."

"Two friends? Who were they?"

"My pocket knife, and my harmonica," Gottleib said, pulling them from his pockets.

# WABASH
## or
# A NIGHT IN A DELAMAR SALOON

### INTRODUCTION

When I met Dr. Joseph Walker first, he was an eminent physician, much respected among his peers for his pioneer work in urology. Because he was a native of St. George, he enjoyed coming back to visit his family and friends and to stop at the Tabernacle, the Court House, and the Temple, as he would say, "Just to make sure that they are still there."

His parents, Charles L. Walker and Aggatha McAllister, had been called to Dixie with the first company. Since they had just finished and moved into a new home in Salt Lake City, this represented a real trial and test of faith. Charles L. was a stone-cutter by trade and a poet by nature. He had a new song or poem for nearly every occasion, until he became known as "The Poet Laureate of Dixie."

Dr. Joe, as his friends called him, was the first boy to be born into this family—after three girls. Better still, he was born on the birthday of the Prophet Joseph Smith, but most remarkable of all, he was born with a caul over his face. This most unusual phenomenon appears so rarely that it was said to indicate that this child would have unusual abilities, special insights, which are sometimes called ESP.

As a youth Joe was especially bright in school; indeed he was often bored with having not enough to do, not enough challenge. Classes were crowded, books were scarce, and most of them worn. He became a clever critic, whose apt remarks and jingles kept his companions in stitches when they should have been intent on their lessons or attentive to the Sunday sermons.

In a letter to him I wondered what had motivated him to go on to school, and to become a doctor. His answer follows:

Dearest Lady—

. . . You asked if any special influence has determined important reactions in my life. Yes. One I shall tell you about now.

I was chopping wood in the woodcamps of DeLamar. I was working for a gang I now call 'Alcoholics Unanimous', because they were all drunks. My woodchopper pal was a youngster about my age called Wabash. He came from Wabash, Indiana. At the end of three months chopping we came to camp to be paid off. Our Alcoholic drew $1800 for the sale of the wood we chopped. He blew it all in one night in one saloon. We got nothing. Wabash and I went into a huddle and decided to go to Alaska where a gold rush was on and pan gold and get rich. We spent the night before we were to leave in a large saloon, just watching its life bounce about us. We toyed with a glass of beer. After all, the place was warm, jolly and friendly, even though a bit rough when measured by the standards of the Y.M.C.A.

A typical saloon piano pounder was banging away at the piano. He didn't know a tune from a turnip, but he was a thirsty, willing cuss. No one was listening to him. None offered him a beer. A bit weary and dry and discouraged, he left the piano and went to the bar. The Bar Keeper just shook his head, meaning no beer, and no more of your playing.

Wabash stepped to the piano. He was dressed in wood-chopper's clothes, hair not trimmed, face not shaved for a week, heavy half-top boots with his overalls stuffed in them. A heavy canvas coat, wool lined.

Then, and gosh-a-mighty, lightning seemed suddenly to strike the keyboard as his trained fingers raced from end to end. You know how a professional does that limbering-up trick. Men stood frozen in their places, glasses half raised to their lips, matches burning in their fingers. Every eye was glued to that piano. Rude, rough, and uncouth as these wanderers were, they recognized a master in this Wabash.

Then soft, low, tenderly came the rhythm of "I Long to See my Mother in the Doorway, On the Banks of the Wabash Far-Away." There came a shower of quarters, fourbit pieces and dollars on the floor and about the piano. Wabash knew the answer to that.

And now he sang it, but with that subtle artist's appreciation of an audience that appreciates. The way he wrapped that word "Long" with the melody of the music created a hunger in the heart of his listeners and more, he made the word project the doorway untold thousands of miles away, so far away that only by longing could you reach it. But the height of his interpretation of the song came when he reached the word "far-away" in the phrase "on the banks of the Wabash far-away." The listeners felt themselves lost forever, but clinging to a strange something by memories Wabash awakened in them.

More money showered on the floor. Again he sang a verse, but now he emphasized Mother. All of those hard, rough, tough men had a Mother. And never a son but loved his Mother, and also too many sons who had forgotten Mother. Wabash refreshed their memory by watering it with emotions. Men's eyes wetted; few could trust themselves to speak. All were seeing a doorway with a Mother standing in it.

Again came a shower of coins about the piano. Wabash was a born artist. He knew by instinct the emotional sag that comes with even a little too much. But the men wanted more, that was evident.

The barkeeper brought over to the piano a glass of beer. Wabash sipped at it, and then began a repertoire of the Stephen Foster melodies—"Ol' Black Joe," "Way Down Upon the Swanee River," "My Old Kentucky Home." Then to rest his voice, he would play a jig, a waltz, a tap-dance tune. Strange, there were men among those Outcasts who would step out and do a jig or tap dance, or several would swing into a waltz. Music, emotions, memories, alcoholic stimulated were attacking loneliness, and in the smoke-filled saloon many plainly saw the outline shadows of Mother joining in the informal party. These miners, woodchoppers, freighters and tramps had by music found a common understanding.

It was nearly 3 A.M. when the Saloon Swamper with a broom swept up the night's gleanings for Wabash, put them into a bag, and handed it to him. Wabash was now the real artist. He sang "Home, Sweet Home!" and that heart-warming song of the Scots, "Bonnie Annie Laurie." The night in DeLamar's largest saloon was ended.

Wabash and I went to the livery stable and stretched out on the hay and just talked, talked about going next day to Alaska to pan gold. But when morning came and we sat in Wong's Cafe eating breakfast of ham and eggs, Wabash said, "I think I'll hit back home and go on with my music and singing. Seems a pretty good way to pan gold to me."

And soon I saw Wabash on a freight wagon, Milford bound, and Wabash bound to continue his studies. He had over 300 dollars in silver in his pockets.

I was left alone in DeLamar, jobless, wondering, wondering; wondering if maybe there wasn't something better than chopping wood at $2.00 a day. Maybe, I thought, if something happened to me to knock loose something inside myself, a better way of life than living with Alcoholics could be found.

Wabash drove away. I went to the Post Office. Wonderful to go to the Post Office when you are in a strange place and lonely. There was a letter from Tina. She had changed her salutation from Dear Friend to Dear Joe. She gossiped about her crowd. Told me how jealous a certain boy friend was because she wrote to me, a wretched Atheist, a little Monster on his way to hell for certain. And then she added, "But the worries are all his. I have confidence in you."

The wood wagons would be leaving soon for the hills and the wood camp. I must answer the letter quickly. I went to Whitehead, Miles, & Co. store to answer it. Henry W. Miles came to me and said he was going away for some weeks, maybe months on business with the Masonic Lodge in San Francisco. He would need a clerk to help Bert out in the store. I would get $2.00 a day and could sleep in the back room.

And so ended my days as a woodchopper, and began my days with civilized people and with Warren Hastings. And with Henry W. Miles, who had more influence on me than any other man in all my life. For he shaped my literary tastes, defined my thought patterns, and moulded me out of the clay of a woodchopper into quite something else.

In another letter I'll tell you more about Henry Miles, the lad from London, and how it all filtered through my uncouth make-up.

---

I never did receive the promised letter, but through the years learned in brief Joe's story. Henry Miles directed his reading; he discussed with him the qualities of a good life—

29

the development of the highest skills of which one is capable. He introduced Joe to the ancient philosophers; these the young man read widely and deeply. After a long discussion about "Who serves best, the teacher or the doctor?" Joe decided to become a doctor.

This meant first going to the University of Utah; graduating with honor; entering The Jefferson Medical College in Philadelphia. In June 1908 he again graduated with honor, and in November following married Tina, who through all the years had remained faithful to him. He was now thirty years old; she three years younger.

After a few years of general practice in Rexburg, Idaho, and the farm area surrounding it, with Tina assisting by keeping the records and collecting the bills, they decided that Joe must get additional training. First they traveled extensively in Europe. Then they returned to Montreal, Canada, where Joe entered the Royal Academy. Here, because Tina had kidney problems, he specialized in Urology. At the completion of the course they settled in Hollywood, California, where they remained.

In my last conversation with him, Joe talked again of Wabash and of the events of that night. "It was the turning point of my life," he declared. "To think that those hands that could gather up three hundred dollars in silver coin for two hours' play on a piano had been using an axe at two dollars a day! Maybe I, too, had been wasting my time living on a wood-cutter's level. With the help and direction of Henry Miles, I was set onto the right track and succeeded in following it. But it all harks back to that 'one night in a DeLamar Saloon.' "

# A STRANGE HIDING PLACE

Ann Chatterly Macfarlane had not been married a year yet, so there were many things she wanted to do in her house. This morning she was sewing carpet-rags, with the loose strings in her apron and the ball in a basket on the stand beside her.

Suddenly through the open door a young squaw ran, and pushing a two-year-old baby boy toward Ann, said "Hide him! Quick!" And she darted into the other room and out the back door.

Hide him? Where could she hide him? There was just no place.

But she saw the braves, three of them, approaching across the street. Standing up, she lifted her floor-length skirt and pushed the child under, saying "Sh! Sh!" He stepped his feet on hers and held around her legs. A willow hoop in the hem held the skirt at a good distance.

When the braves dashed in, Ann was standing holding the apron of carpet-rag-strings in front of her.

"Papoose! Papoose here?" one brave asked.

Ann shook her head. "No. Not here. No see."

At once they began the search—in the woodbox, under the bed, behind the curtain where her clothes were hanging.

Up the ladder to the loft, into the other room where they were looking for a trap door into the cellar.

The leader came back and said angrily. "Squaw come here!" and pointed to the front door.

"She go out there," said Ann going to the middle door and pointing out the back one. "That-a-way." And she pointed in the wrong direction. The leader stopped to look for tracks. Sure enough, he found them, but going in the opposite direction from where Ann had pointed. Now he knew that she had not told him the truth on this; she must also be trying to deceive him again. That baby was in the house. He felt sure that it was. He returned mumbling and glowering to pound the top of the bed, open cupboard and closet doors, climb back to the loft again. Then out to the root cellar behind the house, where again he looked for tracks in the sand.

He started away, and reaching the center of the road, turned suddenly and came back to the door. It was as if he almost smelled the child, or sensed that it was really in that room, though he could not see it. He would pretend to go away and then return suddenly and surprise her.

Ann kept on her feet, moving about the room slowly, and when she was alone, talking in low, encouraging tones to the little fellow under skirt.

It seemed an endless time that she knew they were watching her house, waiting to see if the Indian mother would come back, or if she herself would betray the hiding place.

Finally her husband came home for lunch, and Ann told him the situation. He walked over to the camp, which was across the street but facing their house. He talked to the leader, gave him a small piece of bacon which he had brought home for their own use, and so appeased him somewhat.

Though the Indian left town that afternoon, the squaw mother did not venture back for her child until after another whole day had passed. In the meantime, the little fellow made no outcry or protest, but ate the food that was offered, and rested quietly in the arms of his new mother. But his joy to see his own when at last she did come was beautiful to see.

# MARY PLATTE AND THE MOLASSES BARREL

The winter of 1861-1862 has gone down in history as "The Flood Year" for the Mormon colonies of Southern Utah. It was, in fact, a wet season for the entire West, but each of the villages in Southern Utah had its own list of disasters and hair-breadth escapes.

At Fort Harmony the walls became so soaked and wet that one fell in, killing two of John D. Lee's children, six-year-old George Albert and five-year-old Margaret Ann, both belonging to his wife Sarah Caroline, who was still living in the Old Fort.

At Santa Clara there were many narrow escapes but no deaths. In the early evening Jacob Hamblin himself was almost lost when the place where he was standing, a piece almost as big as a house, split off and slid down into the stream. Here he was, his footing melting away under him like sugar, and no way to climb out. Just as the last moment a lasso rope whirled over his head and fell around his body. His Indian boy, Albert, had seen his predicament and come to his rescue. The rope was tied securely to a tree, and Jacob, bracing his feet against the bank and pulling with his hands, was able to climb to safety.

This same rope, tied to the same tree, was later fastened

to the gate of the fort, and as the water rose around it, served as a guide to which each one clung as he waded out through the darkness to climb to the fire and temporary shelter on higher ground.

Families on the Gunlock Creek abandoned their homes and watched them go down in the flood, while those on the upper Virgin River suffered the greatest damage of all. Here the volume of water was many times greater, for this stream drained a large area.

The stories that have come from this flood! They would fill a small volume, but here we are concerned with only one, that of Ben Platte and his wife Mary.

Ben and Mary Platte had come to Utah on the Perpetual Emigration Fund, which meant that they had free transportation by ship and train to St. Louis, and from there walked to Zion, pulling their personal belongings in a hand-cart, and receiving their food from Church-owned supply wagons. In return, they were to give one year of labor to public works, or to the Bishop or presiding elder in some of the outlying settlements. Ben and Mary had worked their time out in Harmony under John D. Lee, and moved in 1858 to Pocketville, where Philip Klingonsmith and some others had established a small colony. This was on the Virgin River across from the present town of Rockville.

The fast-rising stream in the daylight made it possible for them to drive their cattle to higher ground, move their wagon and plow, harnesses and tools to safety. Their furniture and household goods were also saved, but the house itself and the granary with most of the stored wheat and corn went down the stream, as did their barrel of molasses.

Ben and Mary had learned that while the Virgin River dashed through the narrow canyons, sweeping everything before it, as soon as it emerged from the Narrows above Littlefield, it spread out to be more than a mile wide. Here it deposited much of its load. Giant trees were left in the mud, their branches catching other debris. Local people had learned that if they went out as soon as the mud had dried enough to be safe, they would be able to salvage many useful things. So Ben and Mary decided to take their wagon and go down to this point on the river and see what they could find.

They pulled in at the home of a Brother Iverson at Littlefield, where they would rest and bait their team. They also wanted to learn what they could about how to proceed to search the river. And there, under the cottonwood shed, Mary saw her barrel of molasses!

"Look, Ben! Look!" she cried. "There is our barrel of molasses!"

"It is, all right," Ben agreed. "Sure enough."

But Brother Iverson had spent a day "picking up," and it had not been an easy day. It was a very hard job to dig out the barrel after he found it, and to load it onto the wagon. He was not about to give it up.

"Finders-Keepers," he said shortly, for that was the rule of the river, unless the owner had absolute evidence that the article was his. Ben understood this well, and being more quiet and slow of speech, did not press the point. But Mary would not be quieted.

"That is the barrel Brother Forsythe made, solid as a nut! See the willow hoops, and how he fastened the ends! He was so careful to tuck them under and tack them on solid.

"And all the work we went to to raise that cane, and hoe and water it, not to mention stripping and topping it, and running it through the mill. I helped with the cooking myself, for I didn't want it overdone."

Why didn't Ben say something? Why didn't he just stand up and tell this old guy that this was his barrel of molasses and he meant to take it? Why sit there like a dummy?

Then she had an idea. She picked up a rock about the size of an egg and began to tap at the side of the cork, first on one side and then on the other. Finally she loosened it and pulled it out. Sticking her finger into the hole, she brought it out dripping molasses.

"It's not hurt a bit. Just as good as ever, and that mighty good," she said licking her finger. "I ought to know, I cooked it." (Now another idea.)

"Ben Platt! Stand up!" she ordered, and as he rose to his feet, "Take out your shirt-tail," she said.

As Ben pulled out his shirt-tail, she opened up the the square of cloth on the end of the cork.

"Now turn around so he can see!" The shirt tail had a square hole cut out of the side, into which the cloth in her hands fitted perfectly, the plaid lines an exact match.

"O.K., O.K.," said Brother Iverson. "So it *is* yours. So you take it. But I get a little for my trouble, No?"

"Sure! Sure!" Ben agreed, finding his voice at last, and they measured out one gallon to Brother Iverson, replaced the cork, loaded it onto their wagon, and went on their way rejoicing.

# THE JOKE WAS ON THE TOWN

Perhaps the most often repeated story of this whole southern area was that of the mysterious giant tracks in the town of Washington. This village is five miles east of St. George, and the home of the Washington Factory, where the cotton that was raised in those early days was made into cloth. This business and industry has many tales and legends, but nothing to quite match this.

One morning after a light rain, a woman coming into the Post Office noticed clear in the damp earth tracks of a shoe the like of which she had never seen before. It was double the size of those of an average man, and the space between steps was also double. She called the attention of the Post Master; the Bishop came along about that time, and soon quite a group had gathered to see this strange phenomenon. Where did they come from? Where did they go?

A youngster ran ahead following them to where they disappeared in an alfalfa field where the lucern was too high to follow them further. At the other end they came from a heavy growth of grass. These were so plain that there just MUST be some explanation. The Post Master calculated that a man with shoes that large must be at least ten or eleven feet tall, and heavy in comparison. Surely someone should have seen him somewhere!

Who could this strange person be? What would he want in this little town? He just appeared at the west and walked to the east, past the public buildings, then over past the Bishop's home, where some thought he had stopped, perhaps to look through the window. The Bishop had a daughter, but there were also other pretty girls in town, if it was girls he was after. People checked their farm animals. No horses or cows gone; nothing else missing.

The giant tracks gave talking material for that day, but the next morning there were no signs of any visitor. Then on the third day, there they were again, this time in a different part of town, around barns and corrals; again they passed in front of the Bishop's home and seemed to stop at the bedroom window. Other homes where young ladies lived had also been visited.

Now this was serious! Children must get their chores done early and be inside the house before dark, lest they just might get picked up. Young ladies, especially, should not venture out alone at night; more, they must keep their window blinds closely drawn. This visitor, tempted, just might do more than window-peep.

Some suggested that he might be one of the Three Nephites, who, being Resurrected Beings, can appear at will in any part of the earth. But they came in time of sickness, or to help faithful people who might be in trouble, or to give advice. Instead of the Nephites, it might be one of the Gadianton Robbers. Hadn't it been said that they infested these bare red hills? Hadn't some of their final battles been fought in this very area? One of the Authorities said so, a long time ago. Nobody knew when it was said, or by whom, but all were certain that it had been said.

On the third time that the tracks appeared, the first one slid a little, as though the person had jumped from a distance. There had been a light rain in the night, so the tracks were especially clear. Some of the young men decided to ride over the river bed and the edge of the hills to try to find at least the general direction. They decided that it would be better if they each carried a gun, just in case. They found absolutely nothing.

Word was sent to the Stake Authorities, telling them that this problem had become so grave that some families were going to move away. They simply could not live in a place which was haunted by a giant as large as this one would have to be. The Stake Authorities were asked to meet with the people on Sunday night in meeting, but would they come a little early and talk with two or three of the sisters who had become almost hysterical about this strange phenomenon? Of course, Brother Snow, safe over there at St. George, could not appreciate what it was like to be here in Washington and haunted by a Supernatural Being. The meeting was carried on as usual: singing by the choir, prayer, more singing, and then the Sacrament and the speakers. It should have been like any other meeting, but it was not. Instead of being quieted and comforted, many people felt all the more tense. A few women wept and twisted their handkerchiefs.

Seated in the choir was the Bishop's daughter. From this position she looked over the audience. Consternation and worry was on every face. Well, not on *every* face. On the back row the line of boys were all looking serious indeed, all but one. Young Ithamar Sprague wore a grin wide as that of a jack-o-lantern.

The President suggested that they have the dismissal prayer, so that any who cared to might leave, and those who wanted to discuss this problem in a more informal way might stay and talk personally with President Snow.

The Bishop's daughter knew well that Ithamar would ask to see her home. This time she would let him, for she had formed her own ideas. He did ask and she accepted, and then as they drew away from the crowd and crossed the street, she stopped and faced him.

"You seemed to be having a right good time all during meeting," she said. "You're at the bottom of this, you know you are!"

Ithamar just couldn't restrain his laughter! It was just too funny! He fairly bent over with mirth. On the other hand, she saw the other side. She'd lived in fear for a whole week.

"You laugh now," she said. "But you'll laugh out of the other corner of your mouth when the other big guys catch you! They'll tie you by your thumbs and horse-whip you, or do something worse. You've made fools of them letting them ride the hills and the river bed after your bogus giant. Don't think you'll get off easy when they find out."

But Ithamar still thought it was the funniest thing that had ever happened. She turned in anger and started back to the Church. She didn't know the secret, but she did know that he was at the bottom of it all, and that it was actually a hoax.

"Discretion is the better part of valor," and in this case young Ithamar knew that he must do the vanishing act. He hurried home, set out in plain sight the giant soles that he had fashioned from plywood. Straps on the top fitted his hands as he carefully pressed the tracks onto the ground, one track to every three short steps that he took, with the giant seeming headed in the opposite direction.

He quickly gathered his clothes together, got himself a couple of quilts and rolled them all into one roll. His underwear, sox, extra shirts went into a white flour sack. Word wouldn't get out tonight, but by early morning, the mystery of the giant tracks would all be solved.

At the public camp ground at the edge of town there were some Santa Clara peddlers on their way home. They would pull out before daylight, and he would get a ride with one of them. They would have sold their loads and surely one could make room for him.

The teams arrived in Santa Clara in the early forenoon. Ithamar was lucky; the teamster shared his breakfast with him. Better still the driver, Brother Stucki, drove to his home at the western edge of town. Here Ithamar worked several hours cleaning ditch, for he wanted to pay for his trip and earn his meals for as long as he would have to stay. That wasn't long. He caught a ride on to Beaver Dams that same afternoon.

Now he was well out of reach of the Washington boys. They would have been justified in giving him rough treatment if they had caught him just at the right time, but now that it was all over, they would laugh at themselves. At least they ought to.

Some say that Ithamar Sprague never returned to Washington in all the rest of his life. Certain it is that he went on south to Bunkerville, where in 1880 he married Annie Maria Leavitt, who bore him six sons and one daughter. He was a rock mason who helped to build the Meeting House in Bunkerville, the grade school building, and several homes. His family grew up in that village, whence most of them moved south to the Muddy Valley and on to Las Vegas.

The story of the Big Shoes, sometimes called the Story of the Backwards Boots, or The Giant Tracks is as perennial as the sunflowers, and fully as cheerful.

# THE STORY OF GRIZ

When this story opens I was ten years old. We had three girls in our family before we got a boy, and since I was oldest, I had to take care of the mail ponies. My father, (we called him Pa), had a contract to run the mail from Bunkerville, Nevada, to Moapa, a thirty-five-mile trip across the desert, making three trips a week, out on Monday, Wednesday, and Friday, and back the alternate days. There was no trip on Sunday.

The same team went out and back, and the trip was so strenuous that they would have to have a ten-day to two-week's rest before they could run it again. They would leave Bunkerville at five o'clock in the morning, and get back at five o'clock the next afternoon. On this day Pa was having his late dinner with "Uncle Herb," the man who took the mail on from Bunkerville to Beaver Dams, a short run by horseback. I had watered the team and put on the nose-sacks.

"Another five minutes, and I'd never been able to save him," Pa said, as I came in. "He was that near dead. I was right where we turn off to 'The Pockets' for our noon stop, when this black object caught my eye. He was in the sand against a little scrubby bush that didn't give any shade. I don't know why I did, but I pulled the team to a stop, wrapped the lines around the brake, grabbed the canteen, and run. I spoke to the dog, but there was no sign of life in his eyes. I poured a little water through his mouth, but it ran right through and he didn't make a move. He was almost stiff when I turned him onto his back and poured another lid full down his throat. The canteen lid holds about a tablespoon full, I'd guess.

"Then I picked him up and carried him to the buckboard and took the team down into the camping place.

"Then, before I even unhitched and put on the nose-sacks, I fixed a place in the shade under the ledge, carried Griz to it, and put my wet handkerchief over his head. I don't know why I called him Griz; it was just the first name that came into my head, and it seemed to fit. His hair is long and has some white, especially on his throat and belly. A little yellow in it too. All the time I kept talking to him like I thought he could hear. Maybe he could.

"When I put the next lidful of water into his mouth, he really swallowed. I knew then that he would live. Before long, he began to stretch and move and look around. I gave him one little bite of bread, and knew I had won! He'd live now, for sure.

"I was so busy with the dog that I was late getting on the road again, so I didn't even stop to go back and see which way he was traveling. I didn't pass anyone coming this way; I think his outfit was going towards Las Vegas. The dog had pretty run himself out before he was overcome by the heat, I'd guess."

During all this, Herb made no comment, but now he spoke firmly.

"Don't even try to find his owner!" he said. "He's your dog now. You saved his life. In another hour the crows would have been tearing him apart. A dog lost on the desert is *really* lost."

I was so happy to hear Herb say that, so relieved that Pa agreed with him. Griz could be our very own dog for the rest of his life. Pa figured that he was less than a year old, but would grow to be a large dog. His eyes were not the same color, either, one was blue and the other yellow. But we didn't mind.

"Where did you get that ugly dog," a fellow asked our four-year-old one day.

"Old Griz is a better dog that you is!" the child answered promptly. It was so with us all; no one could ridicule our dog!

We never grew tired of wondering about his past. Was he the pet of little children? And had they cried to lose him? Maybe they had prayed to the Dear Father in Heaven to help Griz, and that is why Pa saw him in the first place. He could so easily have passed him up. His former owners would be glad that he had a home where he was loved so much. Was he born in Los Angeles? Or had he come from Salt Lake City, or maybe from some big city far, far away. If his former master came, would Griz remember and want to go back? We spent a lot of time at this "Guessing about Griz" game. One thing was sure, he didn't know anything about the desert animals, and he didn't even bark at the cat. They just ignored each other, as though each was a little jealous.

From the first, Griz loved the baby, who was just venturing to walk alone a little. The two older boys worked out a game of "Hide the baby." One would hold Griz and blindfold him, while the other would hide the baby. Then they'd turn the dog loose with the order, "Find the baby!" and Griz would smell his way and search until he located the hiding place, when he would give a short, sharp bark.

This game paid out well, for by the next spring when the baby could really run away, Griz was his self-appointed guard. One day he had crossed the street and was going up the sidewalk, past where several loafers that we called the "spit-and-whittle gang" were sitting.

"I dare any one of you to pick that child up," one of the men said.

Another stood to take the dare and reached toward the baby, but Griz growled and the hair on his neck stood up until the man stepped back. Then there was the time when the baby was really lost, and we were all looking for him. We found him on the bank of the Big Ditch trying to reach the water with his toes, and Griz holding him back with a firm grip on his little pants!

A member of this same "Spit-and-Whittle" crowd told of an incident where Griz protected the baby unknown to any family member. Let him tell it:

"One forenoon when we wuz a-settin' there, we saw the little feller come out the gate and start across the street to the corral. As usual, the dog was alongside. They got right in the middle of the road when that wild old range cow—Old Two-Bucks, I think you called her—well, she come out, and started like she was goin' to look the kid over herself.

"You'd never believe the show that dog put on! He kept between the baby and the cow; he barked, he nipped at her nose, he dodged under her horns and snapped at her legs—all the while keeping her attention away from the baby. Better'n a ring-side seat at a bull killin', that wuz.

"The dog had it practically won, but Zeke couldn't stand the suspense. He picked up a rock about the size of a hen's egg, and let fly as hard as he could. He's had the reputation of bein' as true with a rock as any man with a gun. He got her on the shoulder just at the base of her neck with such a bang that she lost all her interest in the kid and lit out on a dead-run down the street."

## In The Spring

Spring brought many new experiences to Griz, for he went with me each evening to get the cows. By this time our stack of last year's hay would be gone, or so nearly gone that we must save it for the mail ponies. The early rains meant that for a few weeks there would be grass and flowers enough in the hills to feed the cows. True, the milk would taste of some of the weeds, but the butter would be extra sweet and yellow. So it was that every morning after they were milked, the cows would be driven out, across the Big Ditch, and into the foot-hills.

Now spring is the time for baby calves, so we could be sure that the cows would come home to feed their babies, and also to unload their heavy udders. But often they would wait until dark before they remembered. So I would get on Selah, my own little pony, and with Griz along for company, would ride into the hills to find the cows. For a few weeks, this was my regular evening chore.

It was something of an adventure to cross the Big Ditch, that magic line which divided the town from the desert. Below the ditch were homes with shady trees, gardens of flowers and vegetables, fields and orchards, all watered by sub-ditches and spreading out to ever smaller ones all over the valley. The Big Ditch was really our life-stream. Let it be empty for a season and everything would be dead.

Across the ditch the low hills stretched back to a high mountain wall. On these low hills grass would spring up from the January and February rains, most of it under the shelter of scraggelty bushes or cactus or just chaparral. No animal—no cow, at least—could eat any of these; they could only reach for the clumps of grass near them.

Spring on the desert is all the more beautiful because it is so short. The little annual flowers, buttercups, verbenias, slippery-Ellens, come first, with Indian paints a little later and blue soldiers along with the other brush. The cactus bloom after the heat begins and the little ground-flowers begin to wilt. Such vivid colors in those cactus roses! But such a lot of thorny protection, too! Even the prettiest of the *Arizona Highways* pictures cannot do justice to these. Then, last of all, the tall stems of the yucca and Joshua tree open in heavy, waxen bells. "Candles of the Lord" some early travelers named them, and the name fits perfectly.

Through the heat of the day, nothing moves on the desert, then as the sun gets low in the west and through the long, long twilight animals begin to stir. Griz was full of curiosity, running here and there with his nose to the ground. A big jack-rabbit jumped up right in front of him, and Griz leaped instantly at it, encouraged by my lusty, "Sic-im, Griz! Sic-im!" which, of course meant, "Go after him, Griz; catch him if you can!"

For the rabbit, this was a joke; it would take a faster, more experienced dog than Griz to frighten him. In just a few long leaps, his black tail was out of sight and Griz ready for something else, a lizard, maybe, or better still, a little kangaroo rat. This little animal is one of the most interesting in all the world, for it can live for months without a drink of water. Its little body machine is geared to use the same water over and over again! Isn't that strange?

Then at another time, a coyote jumped up right in front of us. Griz gave chase, and I encouraged him with the regular call, "Sic-im, Griz."

Griz started on a dead run, but in just a minute or two he came charging back faster than he had left, and came right close to the pony. Then, just over the brow of the hill the coyote stopped and looked at his, his pointed ears up sharp and his mouth open, tongue hanging out in a big grin! "I'm not afraid of you," he seemed to be saying.

That night when I told Pa about the incident, he said, "Griz was just smart! It's a coyote trick to lure a dog away from its master, and then turn and attack him. Don't ever encourage Griz to chase a coyote again, at least not until he is older. Even then, he'd have nothing to gain except a hard fight."

At another time Griz discovered a turtle, and barked lustily until I should come and see what he had found. The turtle had only gone back into his house to wait, but when I started to talk to Griz and explain that he should leave the strange animal alone, the turtle came out again and hurried away with more speed than I had ever seen one muster before. Another remarkable and interesting animal, the turtle!

I hated to see these evening excursions end. It was so pleasant to climb to the top of the hill and ride along, stopping to listen for Old Brock's bell, and watch the sun go down and the evening come. I had memorized Longfellow's poem about

> The day is done, and the darkness
> Falls from the wings of night
> As a feather is wafted downward
> From an eagle in its flight—

and I often repeated it, but I wished I could explain to Mr. Longfellow that here in the desert the darkness does not *fall;* it seems to rise from the valley almost as if it were being breathed out of the ground. On my horse on the hill-top, I was in the light long after the valley below was dark.

## OUR SCHOOL

After the grass in the hills was gone, we took the cows to the pasture, and we'd have to milk early and hurry back or I'd be late for school. At half-past-eight the big bell outside would be rung long and loud, and at five-minutes-to-nine the Principal rang a hand bell to call the children from the playground. Each of the three teachers had her own door, but all followed the same pattern. The students lined up to correspond with their place in the room (and the line must be straight). Then we marked time until all were in step. On the order, each line marched in; the students stood each beside his seat until all were in place, and at the order, "Turn! Sit!" we all were where we belonged until recess. No student moved from his place without permission.

## SELAH

During this time I rode Selah to the field, with Griz along. I must not run the cows or hurry them too fast, but I could gallop all the way home, and both Selah and Griz enjoyed the race.

Right here I think I should explain about my pony, Selah, for she and Griz were right good friends. I didn't know how it was that she was named *Selah,* but that was the name she came to us with, and I liked it. It came from the Bible, I knew; many times I saw it in the Psalms. I tried to learn its meaning, but no one seemed sure. Did it mean a word of approval, such as *Amen* or *So Let it Be?* Or did it mean a pause in the singing where the harps would do an interlude? Or did it mean to repeat the last line? I didn't care. To me it meant a dappled pony with a flaxen mane and tail, that belonged to me, that would come when I called and carry me where I wanted to go.

After school closed, we could take what time we wanted after the cows were in the pasture; we could play in the river bottom, we could rob blackbirds' nests in the slough, for they came here by the thousands to winter. In general, I was against robbing any nests at all. I'd rather watch the parents build the nest, and then later watch them carry food to their babies.

## THE QUAIL

One day we were walking through the stubble when a quail flew out almost in Griz's face, and began flapping around like her wing was broken. Griz at once started after her, but I stood stock-still. I knew that she had put on this show because we were too near her nest and she wanted to lead us away. I let Griz go, but just stood still in my tracks and looked around. Sure enough, there was the nest almost within reach with at least thirteen eggs in it. I didn't go near or touch an egg, for I knew the mother bird would desert the nest if the eggs had been handled. I did stick a sharp stick up in the ground to show me where the nest was. Then I could sort-of check and see when the babies hatched. The babies left the nest at once, as soon as the last was out of its shell, for the mother bird could not carry food to so many.

Within a few days the nest was empty; every egg had hatched. We all felt that quail should be protected; hunters even should not shoot too many. The real enemy of the quail was not the hunter, though, it was the trapper.

## GRIZ HAS REAL TROUBLE

These trips to the field were the joy of Griz's life. He saw everything, and he liked everything he saw. One day he chased after a little black animal about the size of a cat, but with a white stripe and a bushy tail. Griz charged right up to it when PHIEW!!! The skunk let loose both barrels right into his face!

Poor Griz! Poor Griz! He crawled back under a big tamarack bush and lay with his head between his front paws and his eyes closed. That horrible smell! Could that spray have been poison? Might it put his eyes out? I didn't try to coax him out; I didn't want to contaminate myself any more than I was. I went on down through the river bed and turned the cows into the pasture. As I shut the gate, I noticed the shovel standing beside it. Suddenly I remembered that someone had buried a boy's clothes—or was it the boy *in* his clothes—to kill the skunk smell.

Then Charles came along and I told him my problem. He had smelled the skunk already, and he knew the answer.

"It's the only thing to do," he said firmly. "Soap and water don't do no good; and it takes weeks for it just to wear itself out. Come on, let's get at it. I'll dig a hole here in this river sand and you go get Griz and bring him down. Here, take this rope."

I went back to the tamarack bush and tried to coax Griz out, but he was sick and didn't want to move. At least he wouldn't move. I didn't blame him much, but I really did want to help him.

"O.K. so you don't want to come? Well, you're going to, whether you want to or not," I threatened. I crawled in to where he was and put the rope with a loose slip-knot around his neck. I had to really pull hard to make him move at all, but finally he did come, across the shallow stream to the sand bank where Charles had a place all ready, with a big pile of sand at the side.

Griz got into the hole without much trouble and we pushed the sand in all around and over him right up to his ears. I even rubbed some around his ears and on his face. In a few minutes he came out and shook the sand all out of his hair. After he had rested a while, we put him into the second hole and repeated the performance.

By the time we had buried Griz once more, we were all tired of the game. The smell was nearly all gone, we told each other, and he would air out on the way home. But Griz still felt disgraced or sick, for he followed along dejectedly and crawled way back under the porch, where he stayed all day.

## THE SPRING ROUND-UP

Griz had been with us more than a year before Pa took him on the Spring Round-up. Nobody in our town had a big herd of cattle on the range, but several had a few head, so the men all went together for a few days to round-up all the stock on the lower river. They had a large corral about five miles from town where they would bring all in that vicinity to brand and mark the calves and check on the general condition of all the others. They would turn them loose again, and bring those nearer in to the big town corral to treat in the same way. This would mean camping out two nights.

Such a bellowing and bawling as they made as they came into town! The cowboys sternly sent all children back into their own yards, but in spite of that, some of the boys would be perched on the corral fence during the whole proceedings.

Griz stopped off at the house as they passed, the tiredest dog you ever saw. His feet were sore; he was so weary!

"Take care of Griz!" Pa called to us. "Give him a drink and feed him. He's had a pretty rough time these last two days."

Griz gulped his food and water and again crawled back under the porch, where he paid no attention to any of us. When Pa came and called him, he limped out. At Pa's praise and petting and general mauling, he brightened right up. "He's worth two cowboys!" Pa said. "He's earned his board and keep for the whole year on this one trip."

The fall round-up was not so hard. The cowboys brought in only the two-year-olds that they were going to sell, or maybe a few cows to winter in the fields. Griz went again gladly, and again Pa was so good to him and praised him, patting and shaking and mauling him so much that Griz could hardly contain himself.

"He's worth more than any two cowboys," Pa said again.

"He knows what you mean when you tell him what to do, and he does it."

## THE MESSENGER

The years passed quickly. Pa's mail contract was finished; the mail was now brought in by automobile from St. Thomas instead of Moapa. The mail ponies were sold; Pa had half ownership of the one threshing machine in the valley; the annual cattle sale provided necessities. And we had a ranch sixteen miles away in the mountain to the south, at what we called Cabin Spring or just The Cabin, where we had a young orchard. It was so hot in Bunkerville; our only fruits were figs, grapes, pomegranates, and the finest of melons—if they can be called fruit. But Ma craved peaches and plums, apples and pears, all of which did very well at The Cabin.

So in early spring a part of the family would go to The Cabin to water the trees, clear out last year's weeds, and plant a vegetable garden. Everyone liked to stay in the cool mountain retreat, so we took turn about until the fruit was ready to bottle or dry, when Ma made headquarters there, leaving one or another of us older girls and a couple of youngsters to look after things in town. After all, there were ten children to divide in two places, and Pa had his major interest in town. Altogether things worked out well for all of us.

Then those of us who were at The Cabin had real trouble. Our Mother got sick! This was something different; not one of us had ever seen Ma sick before, except when she had a new baby, and that wasn't really being sick. Pa had migraine headaches; that is, he had one or two that we could remember, when he groaned with pain and took medicine. But Ma! She was always up early and in the garden or at the kitchen, singing at her work, singing in the evenings as she played her guitar out on the porch or before the fireplace.

Now here she was crying and groaning with pain, not able to move off the bed, not able to even tell us what we could do to help her. We had been picking peaches in the early afternoon when she left, saying that she would go on to the house now, and for us to come when we had that tree finished.

It was sundown when we came in and found her so sick; there was no way to get help before tomorrow night at the earliest, and Ma just might not last that long.

"Fix their supper and get the young ones to bed," Ma said between groans, "and you two older ones stay here with me."

It was a sad supper, but little children must eat if they are going to sleep well. Usually each said his own private prayer at his own bedside, but tonight they kneeled one at a time beside Ma's bed and asked the Dear Father in Heaven to bless Ma, that she should feel better and be well in the morning. That done, they went to bed and to sleep.

In all this I had no thought of Griz. I did what I could, gave Ma a drink of water and an Indian Root Pill, which was the only thing we had here—just a mild laxative rarely used. A sip of hot milk toast was all she would take, but she did seem to be easier.

Griz knew that we were in serious trouble; he knew Pa should be here, so he started out to get him.

Just before midnight Pa was wakened by Griz at his bedside. (In Bunkerville everyone slept out of doors during the summer; it was impossible to sleep in the house.) Griz licked Pa's face and whined. Instantly Pa sat up.

"Griz!" he said, "What are you doing here? Is there trouble at The Cabin?"

Griz whined again and started across the street to the corral.

"He told me just as plain as if he had used words," Pa always said, as he explained his night trip to The Cabin. "He wouldn't settle down or eat a bite until he could see that I was leaving."

Pa went back to the house to report his plans and give instructions.

"Griz has come to tell us that there is something wrong at The Cabin, and I'm leaving right now to go up. You take care of the dog and the other chores here. I don't know just when I'll be back."

After he had saddled and mounted the horse, he turned to Griz.

"You stay here and take care of things. Go back, that's a good dog." And Griz obeyed.

Pa was anxious to get to the family in the mountains as soon as he possibly could, but he understood horses. He knew that the surest and fastest way would be to start out easy. It was only sixteen miles, but they were steep, climbing miles. He must take these at a walk much of the way—on the little level stretches he could trot, but there was no galloping. He stopped at The Cabin gate just before daylight.

Ma had passed a fair night, and was feeling a little better, but what a relief it was to her and to us all to have Pa here. And we all marveled that Griz should be so understanding. If I had taken him to the gate and pointed down the valley and said, "Go home, Griz! Go home and bring Pa!" I feel sure that he would have obeyed my order, but to think of it himself and act on his own initiative—well, that is something else again.

So the years pass and the children grow up and go off to school and get married and move into different states. But Griz stayed home, growing old himself with Pa. Each day they went out somewhere together, Pa on his horse and Griz by his side. When the time came that Pa had to climb onto a cottonwood stump in order to mount the horse, he still rode. He was on a horse and called at the home of his sister who lived there—without dismounting, of course; she came out into the dooryard. Griz was along.

*Griz*

Only that day a city official had called at the house to tell Pa that there was concern about rabies in town, and they had been asked to have all dogs killed that could not be tested. Griz was one that should go. He was so old that he might become dangerous.

"I could shoot you a lot easier than I could shoot that dog," Pa said.

Who made away with Old Griz, the family never knew. We knew only that he was gone, and we all wished that we could have buried him and placed on his grave **GRIZ** clearly painted on a neat marker. But we could not. We can only remember and repeat the stories of our favorite pet.